Do It Right!

JOURNEY, MIGRATION & SURVIVAL

GOLD DUST

authorHOUSE®

AuthorHouse™
1663 Liberty Drive
Bloomington, IN 47403
www.authorhouse.com
Phone: 1 (800) 839-8640

Published by AuthorHouse 09/16/2019

ISBN: 978-1-7283-2681-8 (sc)
ISBN: 978-1-7283-2679-5 (hc)
ISBN: 978-1-7283-2680-1 (e)

Library of Congress Control Number: 2019913745

Print information available on the last page.

Contents

Disclaimer

*A*s much as efforts have been made to remove all errors and typos it cannot be guaranteed that this book will be free of such. For this we apologise and appreciate your understanding and tolerance.

Additionally, The migration information in the text has been taken from the US website and as such is not based on the writers personal source. References have been made available for further research and verification of the various topics.

Dedication

*J*rv, Chelle, Mali, Anais, Monica, Dawn, Genevieve, Aggie, Raquel, R. Miller, Sis Pierce, Bro Samson, D Bennett, Joseph, Junior, Rachel F. Elvira, Joyce, Sarah, Jean.

Acknowledgement

S pecial thanks is extended to all my supporters, readers, publishers and editors.

Thank you and appreciation goes to the US immigration department who made it possible for me to obtain citizenship.

Grateful thanks is extended to all my colleagues past, present and future.

Thanks to all my associates, family, friends and confidantes.

It takes a country to get it right and I couldn't have done it without every single one of you!

Preface

*T*he idea for this book came to me while engaging in my hobby of creative writing. My first book was poetry. It was done in trial and error. Some individuals liked it but that was it. I had written a number of short stories and anecdotes related to lifestyle in New York City. One day it dawned on me that many individuals could benefit from reading a book that captures a holistic view of migration from different countries to the United States. The task of moving from one country to another may appear a daunting one to many. However if the correct steps are followed the process can be quite comprehensive.

The name 'Do it right' was chosen for this book as it aptly takes the reader through a process which starts with a vision right through to the culminating stages where one can evaluate or reflect on the journey itself. Despite taking many photographs as memories of my journey, writing it into a book also serves as a resource to benefit an international audience, especially as it relates to the United States of America (USA). A look at the challenges faced from the time I decided what my destination would be to moving to one of the most popular cities in the United States of America (USA) is a captivating and intriguing journey even to myself the writer.

Further research into what would serve to make the journey easier for intentional migrants to the USA led me to this all-inclusive book. The various resources and real life stories captures life's adventures and challenges from the continent of Europe to the United States of America. People from any location in the world can adapt the general principles of migration within this book. When planning to migrate, it is best to get an international relocation company. This is especially crucial when planning to relocate over a vast distance or to another continent for an elongated period of time. My migration period was seven years. I arrived in the United States with one suitcase, which, resulted in me having to purchase most basic resources needed for daily living. This proved to be very costly on both ends.

There is a lot to do and much to manage when making such a move. Such as planning, customs dates to remember, storage, shipping, finding accommodation and also settling in. But most important is deciding how to get into the USA legally and for this there are s many avenues, which can be explored. Almost anyone can enter the USA legally with proper planning.

Let us look at New York City to be precise. Such a city known for its diversity in ethnicity and culture would probably be the best choice for relocating. It is said to be a melting pot of cultures defined through various activities, museums, parks, stores, restaurants, and theatres where you could meet up with people of various countries, experience unique cuisine and products from all over the world, listen to international music and even watch foreign films.

It is no surprise then, that New York City is home to and the headquarters of one of the world's most significant international organization: The United Nations. It could be said that the city is in itself a live united nation.

Why do we need to follow guidelines? Guidelines serve to make our pathways more comprehensive!

Who is this book for?

The contents of this book create an interesting read for any individual who wants to learn more about the subject of migration. It is undoubtedly a resource for those who plan to move to the United States. The general principle of planning ahead and doing the relevant research for a seamless move is applicable to any country. There are important points to consider before moving. The purpose is to reduce surprises and expenses not anticipated or prepared for. This resource can also be useful to individuals who have already moved but are still having issues with settling in. Being prepared for employment, childcare, schooling and education is imperative.

Countries and especially the USA have recently tightened their immigration laws making migration itself more challenging. This is no joke. We hear it on the news all the time. The laws of the land exist for a purpose and we must adhere to them. Based on my experience I am able to confirm that having a plan in place and knowing exactly what to expect is imperative.

Further, statistics show that more people are being deported from the USA in the thousands, now, more than ever before. The television brings it on the news all the time. Moving to America is not about President Donald Trump. He is doing what he thinks is best for the country. We must do our part too by following the right processes. Successful immigration to a different country relies on purposeful planning and implementation.

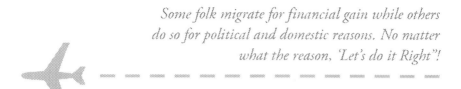

*Some folk migrate for financial gain while others
do so for political and domestic reasons. No matter
what the reason, 'Let's do it Right"!*

Introduction

The 17th century started a story whose plot would never end but would span through time and seasons, even after all is said and done. The British Empire began the story, one that would spin through times of displacement, control of human will, and mostly, the birthing of generations of humans who will be far from their roots, and forced to integrate into a society not theirs while having to live daily with the repeated stories of who their ancestors used to be and who they have to try to become now in order to "survive". Now, these stories are not unique, but relate to people migrating from all over the world. Some of these people embarked on a journey through the different stages of their displacement into a foreign land, namely the United States of America. Some folk migrate for financial gain while others do so for political and domestic reasons. For some there was no consultation, starting from that very first movement way back in history. Of course for the purposes of this project we will not focus on historical movements although brief mention might be made here and there to emphasise a point.

This book, hence, is really a quest into the journey of people in general, adaptation to their new home, and how they try to negotiate their way through this "home" that was not really theirs originally. Integration into a foreign land has its problems but can also have many advantages and this work is a roving eye into it all.

We must agree that life is about humans before anything else, which is why this book looks into the issue of migration, displacement, and settlement. Here we will consider, most importantly, the influence on human lives as a whole, thereby fuelling interactions and solutions on what can be done to record fewer failures and more successes for everyone.

New York City will be used as a focal point into this question of migration. The writer having originated from the Caribbean will also discuss some issues related to the Caribbean itself. The focal point of the book though regards the journey of migration while giving hints and tips of how to create a less challenging transition into the metropolis or western world (the USA). How does one migrate to the USA seamlessly? For those in the USA legally and illegally what are the challenges? Have these people successfully negotiated their way in a "world" that is not theirs? No? Then how can that be done? What is the migration process from planning to visa, green card, and citizenship? What tools and resources can help to create a smooth pathway? Is there a process, documents to follow? Is it comprehensive enough to allow a novicee to follow? This book attempts to answer those questions. These theories, queries, and more will be reflected upon throughout this book. The author having moved for a second time, firstly from the Caribbean to the United Kingdom and later to the United States of America has quite a story to tell of lessons learnt and how migrating can be made easier when properly planned.

Chapter-One

LEAVING BRITAIN FOR NEW YORK CITY

*L*eft with little choice after the volcano erupted I was one of those who left the islands. At this time, the island was in a sombre mood, economic and social activities were mostly down to nil. The tourist economy was wiped out.

An exclusion zone encompassing the southern half of the island to as far north as part of the Belham Valley had been set up because of the size of the volcanic activities.

With heavy hearts most people had to leave their beloved island and their only known homes for foreign shores but mostly to The United Kingdom.

The move to London, the *Big Smoke* was done under a mood of wariness, uncertainty and a certain fear of the unknown.

For fourteen years I stayed in London, enjoying its quaint towns, beautiful Georgian and Victorian architecture. Moving to London wasn't so much of a big change. I had been there once before in 1989. There were a lot of similarities between Montserrat and London in its culture and geography, therefore adapting to life there was easy.

Delicate friendships were made and new areas explored. Having the common language of English definitely made things easier. Though it is known that London has over hundreds of languages spoken there and also a diversity of people and culture. The crowd density was much higher compared to the tiny island of Montserrat. Still there was no culture shock for me.

Chapter-Two

THE MOVE TO NEW YORK CITY

*J*t was not a properly planned move, as I will demonstrate in a later chapter.

According to a study the United States is the second most popular States for immigrants from the United Kingdom. It's not so difficult to know why. The language is similar despite having differences in accent, but it is still English. The culture might be somewhat different in most instances but also has its similarities. The diversity of the climates is enticing to everyone's different choices. And definitely not to forget there is a high job opportunity rate in New York City. Although for some Britain has claimed a name as a centre for academia, still for those going for educational purposes there is acceptance in diversity. Some find the difference in curriculum and the incentives of being on the Deans lists among other things incentives to study in the United States.

The process related to tackling migration procedures is not easy but important. If not planned and executed properly one can run into various challenges that might be difficult to overcome. Further on in is this book I will site some interesting immigration challenges in engaging story telling.

Migration into the United States was and still is very dangerous, difficult and expensive for illegal immigrants. There has been a restrictive legal limit on green cards and lack of immigrant visa for low skilled workers since the early twenty-first century. People from all over the world try to enter the United States illegally and while some are able to get away with it others are caught and dealt with according to the law.

The origins of United States immigration population from the United Kingdom were at an estimate of 19% in the year 2000. An estimated number of people obtaining legal permanent residency in total was slightly over a million per year between the years 2000 to 2009. With over half of the immigrants being females.

Planning: when planning to migrate, it is best to get an international relocation company. This is especially crucial when planning to relocate over a vast distance or to another continent for an elongated period of time. My migration period was seven years. I arrived in the United States with one suitcase and left with the same. This proved to be very costly on both ends.

There is a lot to do and much to manage when making such a move. Such as planning, customs, dates to remember, storage, shipping, finding accommodation and also settling in. It might seem overwhelming to go through all this, personally, so that is where having an international relocation company comes in handy.

Though it may seem interesting selecting a location or destination and planning the move, it also has the boring and seemingly difficult procedures that one has to go through. Time therefore has to be invested to go through it all. I will share below a number of areas to be considered. This information and more can be found on various websites referenced at the end of this document. Some areas, which need to be considered, include:

Storage options: you should ask yourself what do I need to take? What do I need to keep in storage? Despite having so many possessions that we long to take, it might not be advisable logging it all halfway across the world. It could be quite a hassle moving your entire house of belongings at one time. A storage company or a family member with storage space could be engaged to assist in saving beloved possessions. It all depends on what relationships one have with family.

Then there is accommodation to be considered. Whatever you length of stay, you definitively would need a place to settle down. Some may choose to move in with family until they find their feet. Although all this depends on the visa type, which we will go into further on and also on how long you intend to stay.

Insurance: for safety, moving insurance is needed to move your belongings. It is of vital importance to sort out healthcare insurance way ahead if possible when moving to the United States. Whenever I travel I try to buy travel and health insurance at the time of buying the ticket. It's a known fact that health insurance is something of a big deal in the US. Having healthcare insurance eliminates the chances of having to spend a fortune for treatment in the event that one falls ill.

Banking and bank details: As most banks are international you could go ahead and use your home bank account and card when you move abroad but it definitely might incur large fees. You surely would need to make use of cash in the United States so if possible you can go ahead and open a US bank account. This could be done ahead of time to reduce encountering issues when paying for such things as accommodation and insurance. Of course one would have to explore which banks support this and what their criteria is.

There is also the possibility that you might have a pet you wouldn't want to leave behind. So how do you get them abroad? It might be a little complicated moving a pet to the United States but it sure can be done. Find out about the process and procedure and follow them exactly. Vaccinations, passport for your pet and transportation is very important, do this the right and legal way and you should have no problem taking your pet abroad. Also check what the regulations are regarding taking certain pets.

If you are using an international relocation company, the whole hassle of moving might not seem so daunting as their services does cover it all. It might be easier to select a company by asking for recommendations from someone who has done the move or someone who is well informed about moving abroad.

The first step to becoming a lawful permanent resident of the United States is obtaining an immigrant visa or Green Card. There are various types of immigrant visa with various forms and processes to be undertaken.

The number of visa granted each year in some categories are limited.

Though most immigrants receive visa based on family or employment there are other immigrant visa categories. Some lucky folk even successfully use the visa lottery system.

When moving permanently or temporarily to work, school and live in the United States you will need a visa. Sometimes it could be a long process and it's advisable that you get started early on. Some visa process takes up to a year and some take much more. The most common visas are:

Sponsored employment visa; is perhaps one of the easiest way to get a visa. If a United States company applies for you to come work for them, you are likely to be offered a permanent entry. If looking to work in the United States, it's best you get a company to sponsor you and that way it is possible that you can acquire permanent entry. It simply means finding work and accepting a job before moving! In fact this could work in your favour in the long term.

Working visa: if you are looking to relocate without having an employee sponsored visa you would need a working visa. It's easier to be acquired if you have achieved a degree, preferably a master's degree or a PhD and also have worked in your field for at least five years. You could also gain entry to the United States if you fall under the category of their list work skills shortage. To work in the United States, you definitely have to show that you are of some value to them.

Family visa: This type of visa takes a longer processing time to acquire. Applying for a family visa means you have a family member in the United States who is a citizen ready and in a position to offer their support. Though it's quite a stable process it just takes longer. It's easier when you are the citizen's child or married or getting married to the citizen. If going to the US to get married it would be useful to acquire a fiancé visa first. Contact an attorney if necessary to sort this out. With this type of visa one would have to marry their fiancé within a certain time frame.

Now for those looking to retire to the United States there is a lot of issues involved, as there is no known visa available to foreigners without work in the United States. Except of course you win the green card lottery, and even then you do not gain a permanent visa. Though you could get a job and work towards gaining citizenship before retirement if you have that time.

And then there is the non-immigrants visa types. Such as for students, cultural exchange program persons, career diplomats and much more.

Foreign students, temporary workers, refugees and some other categories already in the United States could also apply for a permanent visa and work permit. As usual I would suggest using the legal advice or services of an attorney who understands immigration issues.

Now that you have made the move, you need
to integrate, get to know your surroundings and the
people and services in your neighbourhood.

Chapter-Three

ABSORBING THE
CULTURE SHOCK

When moving to the United States most people only think about the procedure and process. Then, once the move has been made, they go on to make it all about the experience. That's the traveling; the sightseeing and taking in the culture.

What they forget to do is to integrate. So yes you have moved to the United States, but it isn't about you visiting a different country, you have to go ahead and make it your new home. Oh yes, I was a visitor to the United States for many years vacationing with relatives. My excitement with the entertainment and shopping experiences was not the same once I moved in permanently. Relocating there was a different ball game all together. There is the need to become part of your new community and make it your home.

Definitely the sightseeing, culture and cities are worth seeing and quite fascinating but you have to accept it as your new home too.

So now it is time to do things you would normally do back at your former home. There are community events, sports clubs, local pursuits, and much more to be a part of. Meeting people and understanding how you are a part of the landscape is very important. The excitement of moving to the United States might sustain you at first, but as time goes on you might begin to feel left out or have a bout of homesickness. Therefore, I cannot over emphasise the importance of integrating becoming part of your new home. Moving to the United States isn't about you living in another country it is becoming a member of another country. You live here now. Act like it!

As an immigrant of the Caribbean, Britain or any other culture, for that matter, it could be quite daunting entering into another society you know nothing about. A different culture, different landscape, climate and different people.

Let us look at New York City to be precise. A city known for its diversity in ethnicity and culture would probably be the best choice for relocating. It is said to be a melting pot of cultures defined through various activities, museums, stores and restaurants, where you could meet up with people of various countries, experience unique cuisine and products from all over the world, listen to international music and even watch foreign films.

It is no surprise that New York City is home to and the headquarters of one of the world's most significant international organization: The United Nations. It could be said that the city is in itself a live United nation.

A recent survey shows that the city is filled with immigrants making up the majority of the residents in some neighbourhoods.

Recent research shows that there are close to 200 languages spoken and about 40 percent of the New York City population being outside of the United States. Not to forget the hundreds of consulates, embassies and permanent United Nations missions scattered about. The diverse combination of all this amounts to having a cosmopolitan city like no other. New York City is an evolving combination of different worlds with a population of over eight million people.

For close to four centuries, immigrants from every part of the world have become the people of New York. These New Yorkers came in with their own cultures and diverse lifestyles from every part of the globe. New York City residents are known to celebrate their shared ancestry at various cultural sites, performance centers, museums, parades and festivals all year long. They're a number of related public holidays as well.

A large number of New Yorks' cultural sites offer the opportunity to learn more about each and every one's own heritage and get to know more about so many others.

Obtaining citizenship is a simple procedure
but could be a little overwhelming.

Chapter-Four

ACCEPTANCE INTO
THE COMMUNITY

*T*he following information is so important from a legal perspective that it is imperative for me to bringing it in its entirety. Kindly see the reference at the end of this book for further important information. For now let us pay careful attention to these starred items.

Though the processing time for the citizenship form is approximately 6 months, the total process of applying for naturalization and being a United State citizen will take longer than the six months.

So what are the requirements to become a United States Citizen?

According to the US immigration site online, to qualify to apply for citizenship you must:

* Be at least 18 years or older. By the time I was ready for citizenship I was way over 18 years of age, so no issues ensued with this.

* Be a lawful Green Card holder (that is a Legal Permanent Resident). Later on in this book you will read how not following proper procedures and lack of knowledge of the process resulted in me spending an additional five years before acquiring citizenship.

* Have resided in the United States for the last five years consecutively though if you are married to a United States Citizen, the amount of time that you must have resided in the United States consecutively is

reduced to 3 years). Here again one must know that if they are away from the US for more than a certain time a form must be completed. Check with an attorney to avoid any issues.

* Be able to show that you have lived for at least six months in the same state or district where you currently live. Being stable in one state for at least six months is not so hard to do. Knowledge is power and the importance of that knowledge is to use it to your advantage.

If you do not meet these requirements, United States citizenship and immigration services will reject your application.

Be aware that you may also; file your application 90 days before you have met the residency requirement of either 3 years if you are married to a United States citizen, or 5 years otherwise.

The actual processing of your application by United States citizenship, and Immigration Services can take between six months to a year (and perhaps even longer). It all depends on the time of year that you apply, the number of other applications that the organization is handling at the time, where you live, if there are some complications in your immigration situation, and also where and how you turn in your application. This is certainly a fact. I applied for citizenship in April and the entire process took seven long months. I was not disappointed in the end.

As you can see this is quite a lot to take in! Let's continue!

If any mistake is found in your application by USCIS, it will be returned and you will need to fix the mistakes and re-apply. This can delay the completion of your process and increase cost. This can occur multiple times with one application (and would most likely extend the amount of time that it will take to become a United States citizen).

After the application is properly submitted and accepted by USCIS, there are still steps to take to finish the process and successfully become a United States Citizen. These include;

* **Biometrics appointment:** Once your application is received, you will be sent a biometrics appointment notice. This is to have your fingerprints, photograph, and signature taken so the USCIS can run background checks and verify the information submitted on your application.

* **Citizenship Interview, test, & Ceremony:** The next appointment notice you receive would be for your Naturalization interview. At the biometrics interview you will be given a CD and a booklet to study for the naturalization interview. This is where you will be given the questions and Civics test and the English language test. You will also be interviewed about your immigration history and application. You get to find out immediately if you pass the Civics and English tests in the moment so there is no waiting for this part of the process. If you do not pass the Civics or English tests, USCIS will schedule a second opportunity to take the tests, but you only have two tries at the tests. Once the test and interview is passed you will be scheduled within about 6 months to take part in a Naturalization Ceremony where you will be sworn in as a United States Citizen. Hurray!!

You will be able to track the status of your application via the USCIS website.

It's important to triple check your application before sending it in and also try not to miss any of your appointments in order for it to be successful.

Successfully embracing life after migrating involves much more than finding a job!

Chapter-Five

LIVING IN NEW YORK CITY

It's never easy to move to another country, or city for that matter. There are always several things you have to keep in mind in order to "survive" in the real world. What happens after you migrate to a major metropolitan city such as New York? How are you going to pay your bills? How are you going to meet people? Are you ever going to find your true inner self? These questions aren't easy, that's for sure, but we've developed a series of categories that are going to give you an idea of what it is like to live in the city that never sleeps.

There are obviously positive aspects of living in New York, as well as there are some other negative ones. New York City is one of the most internationally diverse places you can live in. The city itself is filled with foreigners hailing from different parts of the world. New York City is a well-known melting pot of cultures. It doesn't matter where you originated, you're always going to be able to find your spot. If you feel like you miss China? Hey lets just head over to Chinatown. Are you from Italy? Maybe you should make a visit to Little Italy. There's also Brighton Beach, which represents Russia, Korea-town and Little India. In New York, you'll never feel like a foreigner, you can always manage to feel at home. Caribbean? Well, come lets head over to Brooklyn or Queens and merge.

One of the things that immigrants are concerned about is language. *"How am I going to communicate?" "What if I get lost? The city is huge!" "What about college?" No one is going to be able to understand me."* It is going to be difficult at first. New things never come easy, but you are going to get used to living there sooner or later, as well as communicating with the people around you. The main language is English and therefore you will need to learn English fast or use an interpretation device to assist you.

New Yorker's are very friendly and open-minded people. If you ask for help they will leave everything they're doing and focus on you. Even if it's complicated for them to comprehend what you're trying to say, they're going to make an effort, and you're for sure going to notice that. Just remember to be careful when communicating with strangers. As much as it is friendly there are hidden dangers as well.

"Don't ever forget about the expensive part! It's best to have a job in hand when you arrive to NY." — *Timothy Scott.*

Every individual circumstance is different and moves to New York City are done for different reasons. The answer isn't clear, as everyone has a unique point of view and idea of what they want. Most people are looking for new opportunities; financial, political, relationship-wise you name it. They want to start over in a new environment, and why not the 'land of opportunity'. Some others just want to escape from the social or economic aspects of their country; they don't want to live in a poor or oppressive country.

New York is the dream of millions of people. New York's popularity is known worldwide. There are thousands of books, movies and TV shows that talk about the city. NYC's popularity has been good and bad at the same time. Issues around New York City politics, culture and socialization are often controversial. This in itself is like a revolving door creating numerous questions and doubts about this beautiful city.

Working in New York

Working in New York City has its advantages and disadvantages. The job market is very competitive. Everyone wants a job and the best spots are always the first to be taken. You need to be suitably qualified and well prepared for interviews. Entrepreneurship is also an option. Later in this book I will give insight into some entrepreneurship pathways and how it works. If you want to be an entrepreneur you would need to sign up for a company. The best selling book, which I co-authored, 'Next Level LIFT: Encouraging the Emerging Faith-Based Entrepreneur', by Williams et.al, gives much insight into the process. The chapter I wrote, "Being an Entrepreneur', is a step by step guide of how to become and entrepreneur, managing the processes, challenges and pitfalls.

People in the city are known to work for long hours. The amount of breaks they get at work is dependent on what company they work for. It is true that there are times when some may have short breaks and they either have a really good job in a corporate firm or work for two or more different companies to make ends meet. All of those aspects and more make New York a busy city.

In order to find a job in the city you need to know exactly what you want, what is available and what you're qualified for. There are jobs that require that you take exams to obtain licensure to work. Do you want to work as a nurse? If you are already a nurse then all you need to do is pass the state board exam or NCLEX RN. Once you pass you have a choice of jobs. The path for nurses in NYC is very competitive. Private hospitals are known to be more rewarding in some instances while City hospitals are known for their benefit packages. Maybe you'd like to be an entrepreneur, or a writer? Then ask yourself: what can you actually do? You need to have experience. Apply for the jobs for which you know you're going to be good at. And don't be disappointed if you receive negative answers or just don't get answers at all from the employers; just understand that there will be a lot of professionals around you applying for the same jobs. You will get a good job too, but learn to be patient and prepare well for interviews. Get help to write your resume if you need to. Do further studies to prepare where indicated and you will be rewarded with a job of your choice. Promotions are possible for those who show good potential and can bring the company more money. That is what New York City is about, making more money all the time. The more money one has the better the quality of life. This is why some folk will do several jobs to earn wealth.

I will reinforce as mentioned before that, preferably, before moving to New York, look for some job opportunities on the Internet. Do your research. Maybe even have a couple of interviews planned out before you get to the city. Some companies would do online and video interviews too, so look out for those. There are abundant job offers, so keep in mind that you're going to get very tired from going to all of them.

At the end of the day, finding a job in New York is not hard but it does take good preparation and the right skills and experience. Be patient and you'll see that all of your effort was worth it.

Once you find a job try to work towards being as efficient as you possibly can. You want to become the best at what you do. You need to be a perfectionist and you should always be willing to grow and develop other aspects of your personality. People are going to notice your effort, and if you keep on going forward you'll soon get to where you always wanted to be, at the top running things. Success will be your reward and people will be head hunting you for your expertise and skills.

"There is no question that there is an unseen world. The problem is, how far is it from midtown and how late is it open?"

Woody Allen

As for the salaries, they are going to vary from individual to individual. You're not going to earn the same quantity of money working as a bartender than working as a guard. Overall, salaries tend to be high in New York compared to other countries because the city in itself is expensive.

The average NYC yearly salary is $69,000. As for the hourly rate it is within the region of $20. Some of the top paying jobs are: software engineer ($98,000), executive assistant ($63,679), project manager ($77,800). There are some other jobs that pay high amounts of money, but it really depends on the company and the employer. Nursing jobs can also be rewarding in New York and varies from organization to organization. Do your investigation to determine the best option for you.

Access to Health and Health Care

When you're living in a new city you should really consider the fact that you're probably going to have to question yourself about some main services. Having health insurance is mandatory, which means it is illegal not to have it. Yet the interesting thing is that if you don't have it, you won't be penalized because of it. However if you get ill without health insurance you will be in big trouble because you must pay for health care services that you receive. Even for making a baby in a hospital there is a cost to that too. Healthcare is very expensive and there is no National Health Service or NHS.

Keep in mind that receiving medical attention is very important for everyone, but it is a personal choice. Most New Yorkers do have health insurance, but there are others that just aren't able to afford it.

Health insurance in NY ranges between $440-$1168 per month, for the premium coverage. It is definitely very expensive, but if you dig deep and investigate more, there could be some places in which you can find the same health insurance, same benefits, but for less money.

There are jobs that also cover your health insurance, so that you don't have to pay it yourself. While finding a job that has such incredible aspects might be difficult, it still isn't impossible.

There could also be some discounts regarding health insurance in case you want to buy it for your entire family or various people at once. It's worth it to have a look at all of them.

You can also receive external help, such as governmental health care subsidies in case you fit their requirements, which tend to be related to the quantity of money that you earn. You can obtain free health care in case your earnings aren't superior to $100,000 yearly for a family of four, $83,120 for a family of three, $65,800 for a married couple with no kids and $48,500 for single individuals.

City Life and Dating

On paper, it looks pretty easy to find yourself an ideal man or woman in New York. More than 800 languages are spoken every single day in the city, everyone has a culture, a different and probably a unique story to tell as well. So… dating should be simple, right? Maybe not if you are looking for quality.

People in New York communicate differently. Most New Yorkers have small apartments, so people get used to encounters in parks, bars, and restaurants or somewhere in the street. That makes you feel excited as a single person as you are constantly discovering new and interesting spots. Whatever you do proceed with caution and take no unnecessary risks.

Nowadays there are hundreds of ways you can find your other half. You can use Tinder, go to speed dates, apply yourself to some interesting club in which you'll be able to meet people with similar interests, etc. There are so many options, and that might be the problem at times.

It's a paradox, but the bigger the city, the more alone you can feel. There are plenty of people out there that want to meet you, but you just feel you're not connecting with anyone. Maybe you meet John on Sunday, Jack on Thursday and Wally on Friday, but the city moves so rapidly that you feel just as if you're not able to catch it.

"The city seen from the Queensboro Bridge is always the city seen for the first time, in its first wild promise of all the mystery and the beauty in the world."

— *F. Scott Fitzgerald*

You'll also have to get used to dating in New York. It isn't impossible; it's just unique and different. Dates are fast. People want to get to know you and if something doesn't fit they're not going to be wasting their time, and you shouldn't either. You'll feel strange at first and that's normal, but you'll soon understand that being picky is the best that you can do.

If speed-dating isn't something that you like, maybe try applying for a book club or something similar if you like to read. Being around the same people every single day is going to give you time to get to know them individually and you're not going to be stressed out about it.

So yes, there is probably the perfect Mr. Right somewhere, waiting for you. You just have to find him and never let him go. However tread cautiously as you would in any country.

Expenses and Rent

We all wish there was a perfect city: a fun one in which people are friendly and communicative, a cheap one with no worries about your money and one that doesn't make you spend that much, but we all know that doesn't exist. It's just a fantasy.

New York is the perfect city because of its numerous resources and social offerings: the night life, the opportunities, diversity and some other qualities that make the country unique and fun, but everything has a price, and New York is really expensive.

Renting an apartment is extremely expensive. In Chelsea you can find 500 square foot apartments for about $3,500 monthly rent. There are, of course, cheaper options in other neighborhoods like Harlem, but they are never cheap. You can always share your apartment with other people, which are going to make your experience easier and more entertaining.

It doesn't matter where you decide to live; it's sometimes going to be a very loud place. It's the sirens, bars, parties, concerts, the subway, etc. It can be frustrating at first, but you'll soon get used to it. At times New Yorkers forget about the noise around them and focus on themselves.

Don't worry if it's difficult for you to find a place in which you can live at first. This is completely normal. You're going to have a very long list of places you have to visit with high expectations. There'll be some apartments that you're going to pass over, as not good enough, as well as there'll be some others you're going to love. One of the best things about New York is diversity, so you'll never run out of apartments as there are going to be new ones offered every single day.

Child Care

Most parents will agree that parenting is extremely time-consuming. Balancing childcare and socializing, wherever you are is never easy. There are times when the love we have for our children result in neglect to our social life. It doesn't matter if you are a single parent, or in a nuclear family unit; or you still live with your parents. You can be taking care of your kids at the same time you work or do other activities.

When you have a little kid in New York City you're definitely going to have to wake up really early. When you have to prepare yourself as well as another little human being it takes time. If you want to get somewhere and don't want to be late it's fundamental for you to leave the house an hour or two earlier. Think about it this way: millions of people are wanting to get to their jobs very early in the morning, so the cabs are going to be full, as well as the streets and the public transportation.

Walking around the city with a baby is much more difficult compared to how you feel walking down the street without one. People are going to look at your baby, smile and let you know that they feel very happy and that they are excited for your newborn. Ensure your baby is with you safely at all times. Remember that New York is a City of strangers with different pasts and history, and as such we do not know what anyone is capable of.

If you want to do some interesting activities along with your baby you can too. There are plenty of forums on the Internet in which moms are looking to meet people around the neighborhood that would like doing yoga, dancing, or just having a conversation with other moms and their babies.

One thing you should really think about and consider even before your child begins to walk is preschool. There are hundreds of different options, so you might want to start your research and look for the perfect preschool for your kid as soon as you possibly can.

The best thing for a family is to live on the outskirts of New York, as by doing so, you're going to be avoiding some of the noise and you're probably going to feel more comfortable. Keep in mind that if you choose to live slightly further away from the center of the city you're going to need a car, but rent and basic necessities are going to be much cheaper.

Studying in New York

Nowadays there are several programs in which you can participate in order to get an internship and be able to study in the city. Being a foreigner in New York might be challenging initially, as you might easily get lost between streets, or halfway through. Being a foreign student in New York is even more complicated until you get more familiar. Keep safety at the forefront of your mind at all times.

As a student, you get to learn and grow with every step you take, as everything is new. Most of the times it'll be the first time you're away from your family. You're going to learn how to survive and rely on yourself. College is definitely an incredible experience that needs to be cherished and appreciated.

Usually students want to go to college in NYC because of the universities that are there. Some of the top colleges are actually there. Some of them are: Columbia University, Fordham University, and New York University.

Most students aren't worried about whether or not they're going to like the city. New York is so diverse that there is something for everyone. You can easily create a network of contacts and important people, as well as enjoy the freedom and diversity that this city has to offer.

There are plenty of opportunities. There are always things to do as a student living in the city. There are seminars and activities, musicals and art shows. You can never be bored. Anywhere you look there is going to be something available for you to do.

Making friends as a student is also easy. Meeting people in college is something that you're going to be doing practically everyday. Some students are going to be from abroad just like you, so it won't be difficult to find a common language.

Even if the city seems to be a strange place at first, you'll be surprised to see how fast you're able to adapt to a new place. In just a couple of months everything around you is going to look familiar. Not let us take a more holistic look at the American education system.

The American educational system is stratified across Public, Private, and Home schools. It is a decentralized educational system which is mostly administered by states and local governments rather than the Federal government. The state governments, through their departments of education mostly regulate most issues pertaining to schooling such as financing, recruitment, and curriculum. As a first-world country with strong values for education, all children in the United States have access to free public schools and are mostly required to attend until the age of 16. For those unwilling to attend public schools, there are private schools comprising of religious and nonsectarian schools which are available for those willing to pay the stipulated tuition fixed by these schools. On the average, the length of the school year is a total of 180 days (although this may vary sometimes) while the span of a typical day at school is 6.5 hours.

Primary and Secondary Educational Structure

Before students are deemed eligible for higher education, they are required to attend primary and secondary school for a total of 12 years. Each of these 12 years is referred to as a grade, i.e. grades 1 to 12; hence, a student is qualified for higher education upon successful completion of the twelfth grade. Elementary school is the first step in the educational structure and is typically attended by children aged six or older. The length of time spent in elementary school span from five or six years after which the students proceed to secondary school.

A child usually begins school in kindergarten known as the first grade at the age of five or six. The regulation of states pertaining to the age requirement of schooling may slightly differ hence the lack of consensus in the age specification for schooling. They are expected to complete school at the culmination of the 12th grade when they would averagely have clocked 18 years. Progression from one grade to the other is based on academic performance. While the teachers are expected to be thorough in their approach to teaching so that the rate of failure is very minimal, occasionally, a student may be required to repeat a grade if their academic grades are poor and deemed insufficient to cope in the next grade after their current class.

The Secondary schools also known as High School is made up of two distinct programs known as middle school, and the second program is high school. The middle school is more or less the junior school while the high school is the senior school. Typically, a student is expected to complete high school (12th grade) before being deemed a graduate after which he/she is issued a diploma or certificate. Upon graduation from

High School, the next in the structure is college or university, and this is known as higher education. Essentially, the progression is Elementary School, Middle School and High School and then Higher Education comprising of colleges, Universities, and Institutes of Technologies.

Again, due to the prevailing educational policy of each state, there may be slight differences in the educational plans obtainable in each state. In many cases, the 12 years after the kindergarten school is usually structured under a '5-3-4 plan'. This system implies that grades 1 to 5 are elementary (primary) school, while grades 6 to 8 are the junior high or middle school and grades 9 to 12 are for the high school. Variations to this plan are the 6-3-3 or 6-2-4 plan. One difference that is noticeable in the elementary school and the secondary school structure is that a teacher is responsible for teaching every major subject whereas in the secondary school, a different teacher is apportioned for each subject.

Funding

Funding for public elementary and secondary schools is mostly the responsibility of states and local governments. They contribute about 92 percent of school funding with about half of that coming from the state and the other half local. Since the federal government takes the back seat in the administration and funding of public elementary and secondary schools in America, variations may be noticed in the structure and opportunities available to students in each state which is why the federal government do step in with the provision of assistance grants to ensure more equitable opportunities for students across the states of the federation.

The three levels of government takes active steps in making decisions regarding the educational policies and curricula in the United States. The Department of Education plays an advisory role in the educational sector. They play at active role of making recommendations to the national and state governments on the right steps and policies to implement to ensure the quality of education is optimized. Their recommendation is mostly based on analysis of data collected on a regular basis. Theirs is an advisory role; hence, they are not involved in setting the standards upon which the schools are administered. Although public education remains the responsibility of the state, there is a provision for the respective communities to also play a part. This inclusion of communities is implemented through the locally elected school boards. They complement the role of the states and also partake in the decision-making process. For instance, the local districts determine the length of the day and the school calendar, whereas the state governments regulate the number of school days in the calendar year.

The guideline for curriculum development are also influenced by the local authorities, although they must be set in line and adjusted based on the number of courses specified as graduation requirements by the state governments. Teachers and school administrators, mostly determine other important decisions such as choice of textbook and classroom instructional methods. Teaching style may be adapted to suit the learning styles of the students in the classroom.

Everyone is a stakeholder in the American educational system. Parents, federal, state, and local governments all play some roles in the development of the educational system. Education is a fundamental requirement for national growth hence it takes a high position in American life. The decentralized approach is mostly for the sake of effectiveness as the state and local governments are better suited to shoulder the responsibility of managing and administering the schools to meet the needs of national growth and development.

Applying for a visa

When you're not from the US you might think that it's all about the green card. Even though I have covered some aspects of this in an earlier chapter I feel it is important to reinforce it here again. It is not that you should worry about getting that particular card and everything else will be solved. Things don't work that way. There are numerous categories regarding visas. You should find the one that fits you the most and be very patient with all of the paperwork and documents you'll have to go through and provide.

There are immigrant visas and non-immigrant visas. There are five different categories for immigrant visas in case your immigration is related to employment. There is EB-1, EB-2, EB-3, EB-4 EB-5, and the Green Card. EB-2-3-4 are for people that have special skills that are required for a particular job in the US.

You're going to be asked to provide official documentation and evidence of the fact that someone wants to hire you. It should be clear that you are suitable for the job and it has to pass the minimum wage and working conditions of the country.

There are also visas for temporary workers, for students, for visitors, for tourists, for employers, etc. The right way to do it and the steps to follow in order to obtain a visa are practically the same for everyone, but the visa that you're going to get and the benefits that it's going to give you is a very relative aspect that for sure is going to vary from individual to individual.

In case you want to apply for a visa you need to go to the National Visa Center, or make an application for non-immigrants at a US embassy or consulate. Most of the categories are going to require the employer of an applicant's prospective to file a petition.

Keep in mind that you're going to be asked to present different documents, as well as you're probably going to be interviewed. Be prepared and do things the right way so that the process is faster and much easier.

Just like most other individuals who migrate from their place of origin, I for one could not help but want to have a chance to visit my native home. Being legal makes this happen!

Chapter-Six

VISITING THE ISLAND

It had been 16 years since my last visit. By now Plymouth, Montserrat was being popularly referred to as a modern day Pompeii.

Although Plymouth has been abandoned it was still classified as the capital and perhaps would be known as the only ghost town capital. Two third of the island was set up as an exclusion zone, with access being restricted and only available to volcanologist.

The government has been moved to Brades in the northern part of the island leaving behind buildings buried in the ash in Plymouth. Many homes, buildings and businesses had been left just as they were when the eruptions started, giving one an eerie and real feeling of what the islanders who stayed behind must have gone through.

A new port was constructed at Little Bay and an airport opened in 2005 at Gerald's. Though the island of Montserrat has begun to recover, its former capital Plymouth has been left abandoned.

In recent times the island has resumed it's economic, social and everyday activities. A trickling in of tourists can be seen daily depending on the season.

After the volcano erupted a lot of people travelled back but the lack of housing and job opportunities limited the number. The agriculture sector also continues to be affected by the lack of suitable land for farming. The economy now depends largely on developments in relation to the volcanic activity and on public sector construction activity. The population is said to be currently between 4000 to 5000; with only one secondary school, a community college, and no universities in the education sector.

The United Kingdom launched a three-year $122.8 million aid program to help reconstruct the economy. Sadly about half of the island would probably remain uninhabitable for another decade.

Despite The hardship, the people of Montserrat had undergone they could be said to be very much positive about the future and are much focused on rebuilding their precious island.

Is this our new home now? Are we accepted here? Are we comfortable to call this new place home?

Chapter~Seven

THE QUESTION OF "HOME"

To those people who migrate, where then is home? More specifically those displaced by various elements, should it be said to be their native lands or the new lands most are forced to make their homes?

This is a thought-provoking question with perhaps no answer.

Do they have a choice in choosing their displacement? Of course not. In many cases it is a necessity that one can easily refer to as forced migration.

However for many there was a choice in choosing their new home and making it a home. Preserving their culture in new lands and passing it on to future generations.

So where is home? Home is where we have accepted and decided to make it our own, integrating, introducing our culture to others and accepting the culture of others. That is home.

The key in planning any move is to set reachable goals and non negotiable time frames. The purpose being for one to stay on track, be focused and very disciplined in the journey. 'Do it right'!

Chapter-Eight

HOW IT ALL STARTED

New York city was buzzing as usual. It never ceased to amaze me how there was always some movement going on in this great big city. 'The city that never sleeps'. An apt name basd on my personal experience. The hustle and bustle of commuters, entrepreneurs, students, you name it, everyone is on the move! Where was everyone going is a question I often asked myself? People rushing from one job to the next, trying to balance lifestyles with finances and relationships. Hoping that, the much sought after work and life balance would be a success. Some even having that dream, the American dream' is putting in the hard work to reach it. Some were putting their health at risk and even relationships. For others it was about the children and finding the right trustworthy individual to nanny that child. Was the quest for wealth and opportunity so important that one would give literally anything to obtain the elusive dream? I want to own my own business and be a success! So do many others. Is this really the land of opportunity? This is still a question I often ask myself. The dream sometimes appeared to be within reach and other times somewhat elusive. Is my fortune and future here in this wonderful land I had heard so much about? Martin Luther King Junior's dream had been realized in the 21st century when President Barak Obama made history. He was my first president. If his dream had become a reality so could everyone elses. The idea being to stay focused, dream big and work hard towards the end product.

I am still pursuing my dream not withstanding it wasn't 'American', or British for that matter. It really doesn't matter whether it takes me a day or a decade, it will happen because I have faith, drive, motivation and the resource not in this book. I excitedly told my close associates who cared to ask, I have a dream.

Way back in the early 90's I had explored the idea of having my own business on my little Island 'Paradise', in the Caribbean. At that time Avon was popular and I jumped right in. I made good sales but my love for shopping resulted in the profits being used on personal effects. Even though I had started a good business trend, there was a lot to learn about self discipline and self control. I eventually put that business venture on hold with the intention of doing some more research and exploration.

My life as a professional continued uninterrupted. I was blessed with quick promotions as rewards for working efficiently and effectively. I enjoyed travelling to different countries to improve my skills and experiences. My most productive periods were in my early 20's in the Caribbean where personal development took up most of my time. It certainly kept me occupied but I managed to enjoy a full social life. Always at the back of my mind though was the drive to be a succesful entrepreneur.

I couldn't help but wonder if America and specifically New York City was where my dream would come true?

I had migrated twice over. Initially from the Caribbean, a forced migration caused by natures venting through an island volcano, resulted in my living in the UK. Life in the UK was a success and career development was everything I thought it would be. I did well in my place of employment and was rewarded with higher level studies and promotions. I had self actualized to say the least.

Many, many years later I left my cozy lifestyle in Europe with the intention of spending up to three months in my country of origin. I had left this island paradise in the late '90s. Still unspoilt and full of life and culture, the island had a rich history of Irish, African and maybe even Amerindian ancestry. Its people were known to be some of the friendliest people one could meet which gave new meaning to the term, 'strangers paradise'.

Living in the United Kingdom had enabled me to realise my dreams of not only pursuing a Bachelor's degree but also a Master's. Where this achievement had been limited in the Caribbean, it was liberated in London. The lack of universities on most of the Caribbean islands resulted in individuals travelling abroad to access further education. The years I lived in London had paid off academically and professionally if not financially. I intentially mentioned the financial aspect in a way to compare with like for like remuneration in the USA. My personal impression is that it is much easier to gain status on the job in the UK than relative remuneration. It appears to be the opposite in the USA. One could invest in the UK but the fact that it was also known to be one of the world's most expensive places to live speaks volumes. Brexit did not create this financial flaw.

If one could link up with a like minded person and share living expenses, then there would be savings and gains for each party. Unlike New York City individuals in London were not as hustle prone but rather more laid back. It is not that people in th UK weren't searching for wealth too, they were just more subtle about it. In fact I have met a few who were perhaps even more given to hustling and bustling in the quest for wealth than some in the US. To say the least wealth or not I was happy as I was on top of my game and had self actualised. I had specialised in my chosen field of expertise in London. I could't thank my maker enough for bringing me that far despite the challenges. In fact those same challenges had been the motivating factors which pushed me to use my talents, skills, experiences and creativity in the quest for success.

Being in New York did not reduce my drive for success in any way. I was ready to reset my goals and explore the next phase of my future. My moto was, 'take one day at a time'. See my workbook in 'Appendix 4'. I knew I was going to reach my goals, all things being equal. It had happened before for me and I was still highly motivated. That day I headed for my little island with a fateful stop in New York I had no idea what was in store for me. Little did I know that a life changing experience awaited me in the middle of my journey. The events that occurred were to determine my fate for the future. There was a change of circumstances. I wouldn't reach my island paradise until many years later. I find it necessary to explain that discerning or defining my idea of paradise from another's had become something of an art form since my social media associates had trashed it. Much debate resulted in each person respecting the others heightened view of the personal meaning of paradise. For me a reference to paradise represents the place where I enjoyed the best times of my life from birth onwards. Some call it home and I do too but many would also understand why paradise is a more befitting endearment to many.

The road to success is not always as straightforward as we would like it to be nor can one make a beeline for it. One has to be prepared to overcome set backs and replace them with throwbacks with comebacks and even potential retracks which I will explain as we move along. Reaching ones goal can be a testing time filled with challenges, peaks and valleys. The key to success is to keep pushing until you cannot push anymore. Keep reaching upwards until you can stretch no more. Bear in mind that success is reachable once you have the right mindset and persevere. One of my projects to reach my goal was the formation of a workbook where goals were set and targets monitored. The key in planning any move is to set reachable goals and non negotiable time frames. The purpose being for one to stay on track, be focused and very disciplined in the journey. 'Do it right'!

My goals had been set for the future. Had I reached paradise as planned, I would have continued on to China to teach English in a University for two years. This was not for penance but rather to fulfil a long standing dream of mine, part of which must still remain a mystery until it has been fulfilled. I looked at myself in the mirror! I appeared to be giving deep consideration to my bone structure and honeyed complexion. I really wasn't. My friend was almost shouting at me on the phone. She was reaching out for support and reassuring at the same time.

It was difficult to hear her above all the noises around. She too had a dream. Her call was to reassure me that everything was going to be all right. Despite the reassurances nothing had prepared me for the next events of the day which I will share in the next chapter. Those events would eventually change the way I look at life in general forever from that moment on.

So there I was in New York City or the 'jungle' as I sometimes called it trying to find that dream. I must own my own house and car within the next couple of years. I must be on top of my career and at least be able to support myself and have a reasonably comfortable lifestyle. My friend and I had simillar dreams. I was going to be an entrepreneur and continue with my current profession. Since I hadn't reached Paradise on that trip, I ended up living in New York City where I had to fall back on plan B of my dreams. People should always have a plan A and a plan B. There must be a fall back plan just in case. The important thing to remember is that sometimes the best laid plans do not reach fuition because the timing is wrong. That might not be your destiny.

A brilliant plan might have to wait for that right moment in time. Do not be discouraged as some of the best laid plans have had to be set aside for later.

I was going to start my own business alongside my day job. Eventually it's success would determine how much time I dedicated to my career or in the future. It is the profession I had chosen after leaving school and had done for almost twenty years. I love what I do as a main job and would always pursue this for as long as I am able. However, my dream of being an entrepreneur was not going to leave my mind and had to be fulfilled. With such a mindset I knew I would win in the end. Place and time notwithstanding.

This land of opportunity had turned out to be also one of distractions. Of all the cities I had visited here in the USA and abroad, New York was the one that kept my brain and body actively working over time. My friend Jade had laughed in a light melodious tone at my comments. Jade was running a successful business now. She had started out in a similar way to me. She had done her research after migrating to the states and made the right choices. Of course this was certainly not without sacrifice.

The immigration system in this country has tightened since 911. By the way that number 911 is almost like a password in the US. It was the key to why major actions and policies were born. Everything was blamed on this number 911; all the delays, the things that needed to be discontinued and those not admissable anymore and the privacy faux pas. The list goes on and on. I had a good laugh when the body scanner at the airports were being birthed. Thank goodness there are no perverts there or passengers would be squirming under scrutiny.

So 911 might thave been a number played for the lottey many times over I imagine. It is a numer that will remain in US history forever. I had adapted the 911 memorial too.

It was not easy having residential status in America unless it is well planned and executed. Better to come when you're good and ready to settle. This is after you have taken care of your loved ones and pursued your masters, and doctorate degrees. No one ever tells you that justification of absence is required. Everyone takes this tax filing very seriously. Who wants the IRS breathing down their necks seeking answers for non filing of taxes? Such a misadventure can affect every decision one make in the future. It is really imperative to get consultants to support such things as tax filing and starting new businesses. Although this chapter is a bit of a waffling venture it actually paints a true picture of the turmoil associated with inappropriate plannning for important life changing events such as migration. Had it not been for these little issues 'Let's do it right', would not be!

Chapter-Nine

AFTER THE GREEN CARD

I carefully fomulated my answer to the familiar question. I knew I was in trouble! I had stayed out too long! What would be my fate today? Without waiting for an answer I continued reflecting on the events leading to my stay in the US. This helped to block out the sound of my heart beat which sounded louder than ever to me. I was accustomed to the question by now. Still when it came I was not ready to answer! I surely was not prepared for the response to my answer. This time it was eighteen months rather than eleven. My anxiety was controlled. I knew I had done what every green card holder feared. The immigration officer had taken my photo with his video cam before posing the question. This was the usual process so it looked like business as usual.

Looking for a matching iris he commanded me to look directly into the camera. I squirmed but did as he commanded. My own private summer or the menopause, a woman's nemesis; was coming on slowly, building up inside me like a pressure cooker. As the heat infused my body I looked him squarely in the eyes pondering for a split moment what the outcome would be if I deviated a bit. I was not a good liar so the only option for me was to stick to the truth. The heat was rising up and I could feel the tension building in me. I had messed up this time. I knew it! I searched his face for mercy! I could have looked for a hundred years! Mercy! That was only a word in my mind, I'm not sure if he knew such a word.

As a resident I should have been back in the country at least five months ago. No one had bothered to inform me of the particular form one should complete when intending to be out of the country for an extended period. Without changing expression the immigration officer gathered up my travel documents and placed them in a red folder. In a firm voice while appearing to be holding my documents up too high, he instructed me to walk across the room towards a small office on the far side. I strolled across the room using my most confident gait. I was marching to the same band from my Girl Guide/girl scout days, left, right, left, right etc.

As I got closer to the far end where the small office was located my confidence waned a bit. My walk of confidence turned to one of uncertainty although still very purposeful, it appeared to take a lifetime to get there. My private summer had calmed down a bit and thankfully I hadn't broken out in sweat.

With a silently prayer I now walked swiftly across the room holding the envelope at an angle with an attempt to disguise it. My inner summer continued dissipating and I was getting cooler. My temperature was returning to normal. Great, I thought! As I entered the room I was ushered to a waiting area where a number of other individuals were seated. They were obviously awaiting their fate. Would they be allowed to stay? I was seen quickly by a respectable officer who in a cool quiet tone informed me that I should have completed a specific form had I known I would be out of the country for so long. He reeled off the name and number of the form. That information completely flew over my head. It was virtually useless to me at that point. I had already erred! He didn't stop there. The question was asked again, why my stay away from the US had been more than a year. My reply had remained constant for the last four years. My life had been set in a particular pattern. I couldn't just get up and go as liked. Today was a day of reckoning.

I had been studying for my masters degree for the last 3 years. The University in the UK could verify this. Infact I had documents to show and even a copy of my incomplete dissertation or thesis if he cared to read the twenty page document. I would finish up my thesis in the US. Well the synopsis at the beginning should be enough to shed light on the contents of the entire document anyway, I reminisced to myself. That shouldn't be a big deal right? Wrong! That was everything to do with following the right procedures. He wasn't easing up!

So I watched him keenly, never blinking an eyelid. I knew what was coming. I had heard all the stories from my Caribbean and British counterparts. As I waited I felt the tell tale sign of my private summer rising again,. It had bad timing and was annoying in its presence. My face was getting hot and flushed as I continued to give my second reason. Can't he see that Im having hot flashes? What is wrong with these people. Don't they understand the impact the menopause has on a lady? Many thoughts were going through my head, trying to find an escape route to what was coming. I remained expressionless as I told the story. Mom had been ill for a very long time.

From the time I got my US residency I had been caring for her. She was a very resilient Caribbean woman who had been ill for quite a while. A woman of strength and virtue. You couldn't just leave her on her own or at the mercy of others. She had earned my love and respect by caring for me and others. It was now her turn to be cared for. I told the story to the officer and my face got pinker as I could see the look of skepticism on his face. I wonderd if he thought I was flushing from trying to mislead him. I'm not lying I screamed on the inside. It's the menopause. Men O pause!! Can't you see? Look! Too embarrassed to say it aloud I kept silent and wished I could remove all of my clothes or sit in an air conditioned room.

Go your way and don't let it happen again I imagined him saying. If only I could take this tighter than tight demin off and this winter coat I thought then I could breath freely. I removed the denim slowly in my mind gaining relief from my private summer would be the best experience I could have right now. The heat was becoming too much for me. He was talking. I was listening but not focusing. I was avoiding the inevitable. Say what you like I thought, but I'm taking these heavy clothes off. He smiled. What are you smiling about? I asked in my mind. I broke out in sweat, not from what he was saying, but rather from the heat inside me. Did he think I was on something and was going through withdrawal? I wondered. Why did this heat choose today to bother me? I only experience these summers once every three months or so. No way, the timing was wrong.

It was usually just one or two episodes and then I was free until next time. The heat had not lasted this long the other times. Today it appeared to go on and on indefinitely. Bad timing I thought. My relatives were outside waiting for me and I had no way of contacting them. Not good! I wiped the sweat from my face. My mother often sweat a lot. I had gotten some of that from her although it only occurred when I was working out, jogging or walking a lot, not to mention dancing. When I got on the dance floor I couldn't stop dancing.

Dancing was one of my favorite pastimes which made me relax. I didn't need a dancing partner to do my thing. The only draw back was that this activity made me sweat. Still I would dance. I was yet to learn to do the electric slide since it was so popular in New York. I had never been to a dance, party or event where music was being played and not heard it. My mind was wandering. I was thinking of things that were irrelevant, yet I couldn't stop myself. I didn't want to hear his verdict. Coming out of my reverie I realised that even though I didn't want to hear the verdict of my over stay from my country of residency, I had to. I sighed loudly and took a sip of water from the bottle in my hand bag. I was getting tired of my own avoidance game. It is time to face the truth.

Clearing my throat I refocussed just in time to hear the officer give the verdict. You must either remain in the US or continue on your way and return here every six months. Noticing the way I was looking at him, he repeated.

My mouth fell open in surprsise. Stay here? Serious? What about my three months in Montserrat? What? Am I hearing right? What about China? The plan was to spend some time in the US then on to the beautiful paradise hometown I originated from, I explained. His face remaind blank. Those words were in my head. Well my final destination was the Republic of China to teach English in a University, I continued. No words came from my lips. My agenda was about being changed without my permission. He said I could leave. I was in limbo. Leave for where? Do I stay or go?

The freezing had started. The summer heat had stopped without me realising it. The sudden cold feeling caught me by surprise. Like it was trying to out do its predesessor my private summer. I suddenly grabbed my coat and dragged it on in a hurry. O dear! What a dilemma. I love New York City. Don't get me wrong. I had been coming here for over twenty years to spend summer times with my siblings and parent. I enjoyed myself everytime. Still I was not ready to come in and stay in indefinitely. I had things to take care of first.

There was so much to do out there and I had things to wrap up, people to meet loose ends to tie up. What am I going to do? So this is how people settle! Settle without any real intention to! It is called circumstance and situation. I realised I was about to settle. I had already booked a career break in London. I couldn't continue on to my island paradise. Everything being considered the safer option would be to stay and do 'my time' or 'settle'. The freezing had stopped. At least one thing was sorted for the moment. At that very point my aha moment flashed through. This is the land of opportunity. I am going to pursue my dream. And that is how my new life began.

My new plans would have to supercede all other plans set before. The courtship period is second to none. I had started the courtship with my new future. This is my new home!

Chapter-Ten

NEW YORK CITY 'MY NEW HOME'

My thought processes were now in full flow. I was never one to let a change of plan stop my flow. Plan 'B' kicked in automatically. A quick thinker I realise that everything happens for a reason. I thought on the old phrase, 'if he brings you to it, he will take you though it'. I had to have stopped here for a reason. I had strong faith that he was going to take me through this period with success. Timing was not an issue, I had all the time in the world. My children were already grown and flown.

I had left a potential love in the UK. The USA was known to change people. I hadn't discussed leaving with him until one week before travelling. The decision was made suddenly. I needed a break from London. We had future plans. Still we were adults and my new plans would have to supercede all other plans set before.

The courtship period is second to none. I had started the courtship with my new future. First my original career must be addressed. I was starting a new relationship with my own business. I had made several attempts before and put them on hold. It was going to take time and alot of planning and dedication. This could be why many individuals always appeared to be starting relationships. The maintenance and sustainability of the relationship takes loads of work and dedication. Commitment and loyalty takes a certain kind of discipline to maintain.

The die has been cast. I am staying in the US. I live here now. Only the citizenship can change that. I knew my new future was just about to begin. I was suddenly jerked out of my thoughts as I heard my sisters voice calling to see how far we'd gotten. We were almost at my favorite fried chicken shop at my favourite venue. We did the same routine every year. My brother in law would pick me up and drive direct to the shop to buy me fried chicken. The only time I ever ate that type of junk food was when I came to New York City. I had to have it just one time. Since I am very particular about what I eat this was my little treat for being good. They had the best I had ever tasted after KFC in St Johns Antigua and Kingston Jamaica. I bought it myself this time while he waited in the car. This was a first and I was doing many things for the first time from that day. I was a resident wasn't I? Almost American nothwistanding citizenship.

Things were happening and my new plans were calling for discplinary measures. Now discipline as far as some were concerned is used interchangeably with the youth. Before time the church and school were seen as agents or of discipline and the sociologists took great pleasure in describing the more detailed measures from a theoretical stand point. It was not quite clear now what I needed to do to move forward. A goal setting workbook (see appendix 4) was to serve me well in the unplanned adventure I found myself in. Do it right!

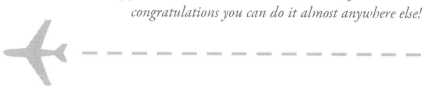

If you can survive the hustle and bustle of NYC, then congratulations you can do it almost anywhere else!

Chapter-Eleven

HUSTLE

*W*ithout hesitation, just like that, I had taken action that would be beneficial to me in the long term. Enough is enough! Still my conscience was bothering me. I wondered for a split second how I would live with myself after this. What was my next move? I looked in the mirror and saw guilt on my face. I should have discussed my issues with someone, anyone. There were people designated to take on these types of issues before you made a move. My sister would be the hardest to convince. She was going to give a verdict the minute I opened my mouth to explain. It would then take weeks to convince her that I had to do what I did for self preservation. This was my life after all.

There were too many things going on at the same time. It was difficult to stabilize love and focus on the job at the same time. One should have been stable, but no it had to be simultaneous. That was a drastic move I had made on the spot. There was no turning back now. I had to face them and confess what I had done. They were going to have a field day on my case. One thing I always told myself was that, if something disrupted my peace of mind to the extent where I felt an equilibrium shift I would quit. Yes, quit! No job was worth my peace of mind.

President Trump was in power and people were asking many questions while others were challenging his presidency. They had chosen not by majority but through their well defined political process. Some thought it was a case of what appeared to be the greater good. Hilary Clinton was a popular candidate. She had given president Trump a run for his money. There were still folk out there who had issues with a woman in authority. For others it was more than that. Still she was a woman and many skeptics were not that impressed with having a female in power. There were other issues affecting the results of course but they are not for this forum. My confession is that when it comes to politics my input is usually zero. President Obama had left the White House after serving two terms. He had made history for America and ethnic minorities and Afican Americans to be more specific. There was so much going on in politics in the US it had become really time consuming.

New York City, being the obvious melting pot of the western metropolis was filled with the hustle and bustle of life and the mingling and merging of all types of individuals. I found it very interesting in a captivating sort of way. I was not new to this hustle and bustle for many of my vacations had been spent in this city. It is only when one actually live here that the real cultural difference is recognised. A city most impressive.

There was always some movement going on in this great big city, night and day. There were times when one got the impression of being in a circus with different shows. Each player had his role perfected somehow. Everyone performing for the benefit of others but mostly for themselves and of course most movements involved money and financial gain. Even presidents have come down from a lineage of migrants to the USA. Most importantly folk are heading towards their destiny. The key to success is ultimately to, 'Do it Right'.

In the hustle everyone is a performer and also a spectator. An intriguing paradox if ever there was one. To be in the land of opportunity meant an ongoing search for opportunities to better self and ultimately obtain wealth by whatever means possible. For some the need to obtain wealth quickly became overwhelmingly intense.

New York City has it's share of employment issues and individuals are known to work two and three jobs to maintain life styles. For some it is mainly a case of survival. Many political changes have come about during the last decade. The last chapter I wrote, 'On being an entrepreneur", in the book, Next Level LIFT: Encouraging the Faith-Based Entrepreneur', gives more insight into some related issues. There are also references to the period of President Obama the first 'black man' in the white house. There were loads of debates over whether he was born in the United States at all. The relevance of which did not directly impact on his ability to lead the country. Despite his position as president of the United States President Obama did not appear to have wealth to flaunt. There was no declaration of billionareism. His overall manerism was one of humility, academic confidence with some hints of humor and joviality. He, from time to time employed a similarity to the fun loving side of the previous President Clinton. Most remember President Clinton for the introduction of a dance among other things. He surely had us and other nations of the world dancing to the Macarena. Still he was a domesticated, faithful type of guy whose life revolved around his family. Mostly a good example to the nation and the world. He was sorely missed after the term in power. Michelle Obama was a phenominal female who gives real meaning to the term, 'behind every successful man is a woman'. A female powerhouse and example for her many female followers.

The nation was fairly calm during his presidency. Known as an eloquent speaker he put everything into perspective everytime. He loved people and was a crowd stimulator. People just naturally gravitated towards him wherever he went. His smile was always in place and he had 'presence'. Employment has always had its ups and downs in the United States and there is nothing significant I would like to note there. America being what it has always been, people has always been looking for opportunites to become rich or just embrace that 'American dream', referred to by Martin Luther King Junior in one of his early speeches.

The fact that First lady Michelle Obama had become quite an icon resonated well in the empowerment of women. She carried herself well in any and every forum. She too was an academic and intellectual who never diappointed when she had to give a speech. She was well loved by the majority. Her humilty and general persona reflected that of her husband, the president. For the Obama's whenever they came into my line of vision, I would get an automatic thought that went, *family matters*. Their example of a real nuclear family was effortless. One cannot dispute the fact that they set a good example. In their own way life was a hustle. No one can hustle like a president who is raising children. Everything had to be balanced because the camera was constantly on them, relentless in its ability to report any dysfunction. The overarching result of such qualities in a leader should have resulted in the American population improving family relationships. The knock on result being emulation by the other defaulting nations of the world. America is a known and respected world power and as such has great influence over the rest of the world with far reaching long term effects. Of course it would have taken many terms in office for such a shift to occur.

Spirituality matters to many but has different meanings depending on who you're communicating with. I was speaking to a young lady the other day. She claims to be a Rastafarian. A religion founded in Africa. She was wearing similar beads around her waist as I was. I questioned her reason for wearing them. She explained they had spiritual implications for her. On the other hand they were a means of keeping my waistline in check. I learned that many associated spirituality with religion.

America, or should I say New York City (NYC) specifically does not necessarily give the impression of being the most spiritual or religious country. This is a surface view but not necessarily the real truth. A better understanding is gained from talking to individuals and recognizing that almost evey single person has an element of spirituality. It all depends on what perspective one is looking at. In fact the spirituality of some folk I have had close contact with, in my subjective view has ultimately left a lot to be desired. That's the impression I got. My interactions with many who proclaim to be christians have left a question mark as to whether true christianity really exists anymore. Even those whom Ive known to be practising christians have often times made wealth and money matters a priority. There are hundreds of denominations in NYC itself. The presence of which did not appear to change much in the spiritual characteristics of the population on the surface. Freedom to make a choice of religion or not to choose is a part of the constitution. I'm aware that many religions have their issues with staying on top of things and especially when it comes to youth matters. Up until recently religion was taught in the school. From a sociological perspective it was seen as a unit of discipline. Of recent times the discussion or introduction of religion in work places, schools etc., is being prohibited. There are guidelines as to what is acceptable or not. One cap does not fit all but knowledge is power and we must, do it right.

When enough is enough and changes must be made for
self preservation. You just have to do whats good for you!
Make that change and do it right just for you.

Chapter~Twelve

ENTREPRENEURSHIP

S o there came a time when I had to make that big decision for self
preservation. As I mentioned in the chapter above, I had to quit
my job in NYC. I did not have another job lined up yet, nor did I know
exactly what I was going to do next. I had experienced things that I
would never talk about. I knew for a fact that I needed to shift away
from ongoing discomforts. I was not sure who could help me. I had
written letters with no result and no response. What could I do? Who
could I turn to? I pondered long and hard on my next move.

One could say that NYC is a highly unionised society. Some unions
were very good and were always making 'noise', marching and having
meetings on behalf of their members. There were some very good and
effective unions, while others were still in the teething stages despite
being established for many years. I'm still wondering if it was me or was
it that my union was just totally ineffective. The thing to note about
some of these unions is that their representatives are voluntary workers
of varying levels. For some it was a peer to peer representation which
did not carry much weight. Yet union dues were collected on time
every month. For me it was equivalent to supporting a habit that had
no positive benefits. Something I never entertained. Yet having a union
is a must even if it was just a formality.

In the end I just couldn't take it any more and decided to move on for peace of mind. When enough is enough and changes must be made for self preservation. You just have to do what's good for you! Make that change and do it right, just for you. Moving to the US is not a bed of roses. On the contrary there are many challenges that one will face along the way. I decided to work for agencies that were financially rewarding although with no union representation. That was going good and I had some income coming in. It was all about survival. I was not yet pensionable and even if I was I didn't have enough money nor was I old enough to retire totally. I was doing a side hustle but that was seasonal. Supporting individuals here and there with editing along with my writing kept me focused and occupied. This side hustle was exactly what it was, it was not going to generate enough income to sustain me, so I started a website and added exotic scarfs and camis. In the meantime I was still looking for a large entrepreneurship which would eventually generate some viable income. I was gifted in many ways and wanted to use those gifts creatively. Apparently granddad was an entrepreneur back in the '50s and early '60s. I was truly surprised to hear this. Ironically on my short unplanned trip to Atlanta Georgia I met a fellow Montserratian and politician who filled me in on the working life of my maternal grandfather.

Known as Marse Joe, my grandfather worked on one of the large sugar plantations in an area called parsons. Parsons is now completely destroyed by the famous volcano, which had been erupting from 1995. This location was home of one of the large sugar plantations on island. The sugar plantations were owned by the British; but run by Irish indentured servants.

According to the very personable Mr. Auk Jeffers, granddad was one of three people who could actually make sugar on the island. A very talented man granddad sounded as if he had been a specialist in his field. In todays society he would have been considered an expert in his field. As my cousins and I sat listening to every word Mr. Jeffers said, I felt a close bond and kinship to the man I had never known. He had passed before I was born. Alas we never met and now I'm learning more of our similar creative abilities, I felt that great loss. We had so much in common, I just know we would have been great friends. So apparently Granddad was the only local on island that could make that sugar from raw sugar cane. Sugar as we know it came from the sugar cane which was grown locally at that time. The sugar cane was planted as a profit making enterprise. Molasses was then made by squeezing the cane through huge iron machines which then took the juice through a heating process, thickened it and produced the dark molasses. I was amazed to hear that Granddad was able to make three types of sugar, brown sugar; white sugar and cane sugar. The other two individuals on island who could make sugar from cane were British plantation owners. The politician gave me much information. Apparently granddad was well respected for his talents. Much have been told of the relationship between Granddad and the owners. They valued his expertise and held that above any other shortcoming he had. Becoming an amazon best seller overnight was a huge surprise to me. Despite the hustle and bustle of regular work and entrepreneurship, I find time to write creatively. I follow a strategic plan so that I can do it right.

Chapter-Thirteen

VALUES

In a place where the focus is on freedom it is important to establish guidelines that fit within ones value system. I decided to share the story below because it happened at a time when emotional and physical needs led to acceptance of the unacceptable. The church was going through issues and the four sister friends were trying to find alternatives to alleviate the pressure. Things were happening and some upstart was calling for discplinary measures. Wow!! Were individuals jumping up and down with that one.

Older folk used various methods of discipline for the youth which are no longer acceptable in our evolving society. Such methods as flogging and spanking are outdated and can generate a visit from the social worker and even police if they are used. Still strong measures of discipline are needed in metropolitan cities where there is much liberalism. Teachers are constantly expressing concerns and asking for measures to increase discipline in schools. A perfect technique for instilling discipline in schools and homes is yet to be discovered.

As to population control, these big US cities have been trying hard to keep things under control and looking normal. Normalcy these days certainly appear to have a different definition to yester-year. Everything in New York is about money, money and more money. If there was money to be made from this particular potential project area it would have been marketted and rolling long time ago. Despite the various money issues folk spend a lot of time shopping. Online shopping for everything including groceries was the in thing. Such a method is not a novelty as Europe or the UK has been involved in online shopping for ages.

Education the key to development of knowledge and potential wisdom was not necessarily forth coming or as accessible as one would have expected. Tertiary education is not free but there are ways to get it funded which has been covered in an earlier chapter. Rationale for actions and decisions sometimes leave much to be desired and books are not being read as much as before. There are so many electronic gadgets and games to choose from that creativity is not as prominent as before. Some claimed that social media and all those internet games had taken over. It is the era of the wifi which gives us more resources for doing things the right way.

No matter where you are or who you claim to be your value system is important. At times peoples behaviours might cause disappointment as we compare them to what we left behind. We must be careful of doing so. Since people's orientation and experiences will often determine their response to a particular stimui one must be prepared for inconsistencies. I will share a story below of one such behaviours based in NYC.

Sleep was evading me that night. I couldn't blame it on the menopause this time. The presence of someone upstairs directly over my bed was keeping me awake. I wasn't sure if he/she was deliberately trying to keep me awake. They'd had a huge fight earlier. I could hear his voice. He was speaking loudly. She was talking hysterically as usual. This didn't mean it was warranted. I had learned to understand her and not be afraid of her. It was something about her culture. Always sounding as if she was ready to have a fight, she often came across as being aggressive. When she tried to tone it down her voice sounded all weird and left you wondering why she didn't just speak in her own voice and tone. Just couldn't get this one right I suppose. It would take practice to mold her into the cultured individual she tried to portray. It is not easy to mold an adult.

She was okay I suppose except for her attitude of having to prove everything and believing nothing. Individuals like that were hard to please. Getting close to them can wear one out and build resentment. I had long decided to keep up appearances but to keep a politically correct distance from her. In her late forties she could very well be menopausal. That can also account for some of the behaviours. Talking about late forties and menopause. Most women I was associated with did not like to use the 'M' Word. They vehemently denied having symptoms. They even went on to describe their mothers and older women as having absolutely no symptoms. There is a huge learning curve here. Mostly though, women tended to be very private about such things. For some it made them feel older to speak of such and gave away their age. Men also did not like to talk about prostate issues which has been an area of focus in male health care. I couldn't figure wether they were embarassed about the disorder itself or the related issues. Pride has a lot to do with what individuals are willing to share. Knowledge is power and sharing is caring. Everyone has to learn how to do it right.

De-Stress

Valuing and living a healthy stress free life is not easy in big cities. Dealing with the stressors of life is not easy. Moving and especially to a different country can create emotional and physical challenges. Additionally as a lady going through some life changes it is essential to find coping mechanisms in order to deal with everything including the hustle and bustle of life. I fell back on many stress relief strategies that had worked for me in the past. Stress can affect every single individual in different ways. Similarly, each individual should handle stress in a manner that is deemed purposeful to him or her. There are lots of us who are creative and as such need to find something to do with our time other than simply sitting around. It is important to try new strategies for relaxation and hence filling that time with things we like to do. This also allows the individual to get some enjoyment while alleviating stress. All the activities below were explored at different times and opportunities were used for sharing with others.

Song-writing

Although not musically very creative I enjoy listening to music and singing along. I don't play any musical instruments but would have been happy to strum a guitar or beat a drum to relax. I ended up writing songs and enjoyed experimenting with different tunes and melodies. This kept my mind off stressful events at least for a period of time. I ended up writing over a hundred songs to date with melodies to them.

Prayer

Forming prayer groups with like-minded individual can be a very useful way of relieving stress. It does not work for everyone but it is an option that can be explored by those who might benefit. This can be done during coffee mornings or Friday evening link ups or however it works for that group. I linked up with like-minded individuals and prayer warriors. This not only helped me but benefitted others as well. Group meetings are great way of sharing ideas and catching up with friends.

Writing

Creative writing allows you as an individual to give vent to your feelings. While writing your thoughts will flow. You might become so focused that you forget about your stressors for a while. I write creatively and have used such periods of writing to relieve anxiety. When my emotions are stirred I usually need an outlet to re-establish my center of gravity. I mostly write non-fiction while reflecting on events I observed or experienced. If you choose to write, you might want to just go with what's on your mind at the time, rather than thinking too deeply or engaging in something new. Writing is also useful for reflection. A time will come when you might want to read through what you wrote about a particular event in your life. If the event recurs reflection on what you wrote can help you to determine what action would work best for you. This works for me even at the workplace.

Poetry

Poetry has been one of my favorite coping mechanisms from childhood. It brings out the emotional and creative trends inside. Poetry is relaxing when you listen to it being read or spoken. Poetry is quite liberating simply because self-expression is free as you let it all pour out. It's for your eyes only unless you chose to share it. Any situation one can imagine gives a reason to write poetry.

Retreats

Not only will retreats, conferences and day events be useful from an educational and networking perspective but can be used as a resource for relieving stress and getting away from the mundane everyday work activities. Some of these events are held in places where there is access to gym and spa activities. Some may have snooker and table tennis. It is important to make use of these facilities whilst away. Socializing with friend and meeting new associates not only stimulates but can also be a useful stress-relieving tool. Do it right and save your life.

Seaside

What an awesome experience! What a lovely sound! Peace, perfect peace! Just walking along the seaside and listening to the waves! Better still, what about just lying in your bed and listening to the waves gently run to shore. For some of us the seashore is no novelty. Yet as we grow away from the seaside childhood activities and settle into adulthood we tend to pay little attention to this wonderful resource. Hanging around the seashore for whatever reason is a great stress relief resource. Try it and see for yourself. With or without a book in hand to read or your journal to jot in it is quite the relaxant that you must never overlook. If you're in the Caribbean you might want to wet a toe or go further and wet a foot. Whatever you choose to do I urge you to have a plan for relaxation. It can be a huge benefit in the long and short term.

Chapter-Fourteen

HEALTH-WISE

J was exploring being a health coach. The US population has dire need for more nutrition diet and exercise intervention. Stress management is a must for everyone but not everyone need or can afford a Psychiatrist. Some are trying but the work life balance makes it difficult to manage what makes the body healthy. What of those people who are juggling two jobs and even three at times? Not to mention those health care workers who are doing twelve hour shifts. The ones doing the eight-hour shifts are doubling up to make ends meet. The result is sixteen hours of hard labor where one can be on their feet for at least fourteen of that time. The lunch break when taken could at times be the only sitting period. To say the least there are some who cannot even take that time since the workload to employee ration is very unbalanced.

Individuals from all walks of life and from every single country in the world one can imagine travel to places everyday. A large number of these individuals have no clue of what to expect in the metropolis such as the USA and London. Many have relatives who invited them over. Some of these individuals migrate of their own accord for business purposes, others for financial gain, education, marriage fulfillment we can go on and on naming reasons.

Those with relatives and even friends in these countries were never told the real stories of how one managed to survive in these tough countries. Imagine the culture shock when they realize that their loved one has been making sacrifices to send a little money back to their countries. One thing for sure when the migrants visited their country of origin it was nearly always preceded by a flurry of shopping for new clothing. Many financial sacrifices were made but never spoken of. For the most part those visiting from these metropolitan countries would have a foreign look, which appears healthy and happy. A closer look and some investigation would reveal that some are barely surviving and maintain good health care is another story.

Apart from a few city hospitals scattered here and there in each state the health care system in the US is privatized.

Coming from the United Kingdom (UK) this presents itself as a bit of a culture shock. The entire UK as everyone know has a national health care system (NHS) which despite the inverse care system provides health care free of cost to all. The US on the other hand does not have a universal health care system. Since the Second World War several attempts have been made to have such a system implemented. Apparently most countries having lost millions of soldiers in the Second World War implemented a universal health care system to create better health care management in their countries.

The US on the other hand had lost hundreds of soldiers but was doing well financially and did not implement a national health service for those folks who couldn't afford health care. As one can imagine most of those people were from minority groups. For all intents and purposes it doesn't appear as if the 'greatness' of America had anything to do with the health of its people. The diversity of the US population can be blamed for this. Looking back one can see that back then most of those countries implementing universal health care had one thing in common. The people were one of the same ethnicity. It has been suggested that ethnicity could be a factor influencing the decision for universal health care in the US.

Of course it goes much deeper than that. One of the more recent attempts to introduce universal healthcare in the US was the Obama care. President Obama touched the tip of the iceberg by introducing 'affordable' insurance coverage. The coverage had a lot of flaws but provided some much needed assistance to about 28 million people.

This still left about 12million individuals without coverage. So although imperfect this is a legacy left behind to support the less off in society. The election to office of President Trump was to see the gradual removal of Obama care. Obama care was stripped open, found wanting and laid to rest as an inefficient resource to the American population. There is no way for me to evaluate the success or failure of that resource apart from what the media purposed to focus on. Apart from healthcare one should ensure that attention is given to their emotional health At all times. While this in itself is not always straightforward there are certain resources including a workbook and coping mechanisms I used therapeutically to reduce stress. I will add those in the Appendices.

Conclusion

The folk who migrate, have they successfully negotiated their way into a "world" that is not theirs? Perhaps not! Then how can that be done?

By acceptance; which is a two-sided coin. Being accepted by the world and accepting the world is a good place to start. Accepting a new world; one shouldn't be averse to that which isn't your culture and traditions. Learning about your new location and everything that pertains to it is the sure first step to accepting new horizons. Perhaps the hardest would be being accepted by the world. Not everyone has the same mind set and there might be various challenges getting accepted.

Overall it's best to take it all one-step at a time
with as much patience as possible.

Appendix 1

A BRIEF INSIGHT INTO THE CARIBBEAN PEOPLE

*W*ho are the Caribbean people? Where are they from? Where is the Caribbean? What is the Caribbean culture like?

These questions should perhaps be firstly answered to be able to understand better how much this book means to the author who is of Caribbean origin.

As to the question of who is the Caribbean people? Where are they from?

It is a fact that the Caribbean consists of a diverse people.

Initially it was said that various tribes of Caribs and Arawak inhabited the Caribbean with Indigenous ancestry. Then came in the European colonization and diseases, which wiped out most of the population.

In present time it could be said that the Caribbean consists of Africans, European, those of mixed ethnicity and the natives. The languages spoken differ and range from English, Dutch, Spanish, and Haitian, French, Creole and much more. Christianity, Hinduism and Islam are the predominant religions practiced but there care small pockets of other religions.

Their ethnic ancestry can largely identify the modern Caribbean people. Some consist of white Caribbean folk who are mostly descendants of European colonizers, Afro-Caribbean; descendants of liberated African slaves, Asian Caribbean, and also Indo-Caribbean (descendants of indentured Indian workers). Kindly note that these names are actually out-dated and the standard name is now 'indigenous people'.

This should give a picture as to who they are and where they are from.

Now comes the question of where is the Caribbean?

Most people would probably only think of the Caribbean when it comes to taking a vacation somewhere of a tropical nature. Actually it's more than just a spot for tropical vacationing. It's a region of quite diverse geography and climate.

As to where exactly the Caribbean is located; it's a region that consists of a number of islands, the Caribbean Sea and it's encompassing coasts. The Caribbean islands are said to consist of about 7000 islands, islets and reefs most of which are uninhabited.

It is found just southwest of the Gulf of Mexico and Northern America mainland. It's usually regarded as a region of America.

Its climates differ from subtropical to tropical depending on the region. The Caribbean is known to have a number of both active and inactive volcanoes scattered about.

So what is the Caribbean culture like?

The Caribbean culture that represents the social, artistic, culinary, musical, political and literary traits of the Caribbean people could be said to have been historically influenced by the Africans and Amerindian traditions. It is also strongly influenced in relation to linguistic, economy and culture by its nearby neighbour, the United States of America.

Caribbean family life

There is a lot of diversity in Caribbean families mostly due to their differences in origin. But overall they are a distinct group because of their multi-ethnic build up.

Appendix 2

TANTRUM THROWING
VOLCANO

*T*he Caribbean island of Montserrat where the author hails from is popularly known as the Emerald Isle of the Caribbean, mostly for its resemblance to the coast of Ireland and the Irish ancestry of many of its early inhabitants or colonisers.

The pear shaped island was said to have a population of about ten thousand before the year 1995. It was usually described as being unspoiled, green, mountainous and somewhat isolated with mostly fertile grounds. It is known for its surrounding black sandy beaches and tropical climate.

It has a mix of Anglo-Irish and African culture and an official language of English. It also has another local language known as Montserrat dialect or broken English'. Although not found in any dictionary the dialect also called 'Montserrat English' was recently published in a travellers guide by the Author. In a sense it just made to some extent an international debut into phonetics and languages.

There is not much known or written about the early history of the island of Montserrat. There is however some theory that Arawak Indians who were later initially inhabited it killed off by the Carib Indians. After a while the British contingent from the mother colony of Saint Kitts settled there in the year 1632. The British contingent consisted mainly of the Irish and English. Later came in the French and then the English who is in control to this day.

The island of Montserrat could currently effectively be described as being quite small with a mix of diverse ethnicity.

According to a study as of the year 2011 there were close to 5000 people of Caribbean origin living on the island of Montserrat.

The island is usually calm and bustling with liveliness and having a surplus sea wind. But this wasn't so between the year 1995 and 2000. On July 18th 1995, the peaceful island was thrown into chaos as the once dormant Soufriere Hills volcano in the southern part of the island came to life. Volcanic eruptions destroyed the Georgian era capital city of Plymouth. By the year 1997, 80 percent of the island had been destroyed and buried under volcanic ash. Forcing most of the inhabitants to flee. The number of those migrating between the year 1995 and 2000 was more than half of the population. Most of the inhabitants migrated to the United Kingdom, leaving an estimate of slightly more than two thousand people on the island.

The volcanic activity continued mostly affecting the vicinity of Plymouth and the eastern side of the island. The author in the book, 'Montserrat in England: Dynamics of Culture', has captured more details about this event and migration to Britain.

Appendix 3

CARIBBEAN CULTURE
FOOD AND ITEMS IN NYC

F or many Caribbean folk wanting to learn more about Caribbean traditions, the El Museo del Barrio, culture and the people, is definitely a place to visit in New York City. Richmond hill, in the South-East of Queens, is one of the greatest spot of New York's diversity. Notwithstanding the amount of culture found in the Bronx. There one could definitely find places to eat a Caribbean meal and almost any other cuisine, shop for trinkets and many products from home.

The United States is mostly the topmost destination for Caribbean and a number of other emigrants outside their region. This is according to a 2017 estimate by the United Nations Population Division. On an average, the majority of immigrants obtain lawful permanent residence in the United States through three main ways: qualifying as a relative of United States citizens, through family-sponsored preferences, or as refugees and asylum seekers.

Between the years 2013 and 2017, the United States cities with the most number of Caribbean immigrants were New York and Miami metropolitan areas. An estimate of 63 percent of Caribbean immigrants in the United States lived in these two areas.

Caribbean immigrants were also a little more likely to be proficient in English than the overall foreign-born population.

With a higher number having finished high school and a low rate of college graduate.

They also constituted for a significant part of enrolled students and labour force most especially in production, service occupation, transportation and material moving occupations in the overall immigrants' population.

Appendix 4

WORKBOOK

W ouldn't it be nice to work from perfect guidelines from every aspect in our lives? It would be nice if we could all pay coaches to guide us to our next level of success? Wouldn't it? Realistically most individuals we come into contact with, will never be able to hire a coach and have to forge their own pathway to whatever success they achieve. It is important to be prepared for the life ahead.

Now we have learned a lot about life, expectations, disappointment, challenges, mistakes, hope and faith. I have designed a workbook for those who wish to develop themselves in a meaningful way. It is important to embrace the element of growth in every aspect of our life. See the workbook below.

Initially the plan was to write a novel filled with romance and anything that the world would embrace. Then as if I was being commanded to do something I realised that fifty pages down all I could think about was the spiritual aspect of what I was writing. It was time to give glory to the most high.

So I started out by editing a chapter from my previous book, 'despite the odds' This focuses on Matthews account of Paul in chapter 25. Having completed that chapter and feeling really good about the guidance I decided to look at the more worldly written novel. I had started with my initial dream which appeared to be trying to become a reality for a while now. There had been a lot of discussions regarding my current situation and the fact that those who knew me had no clue in which direction I was heading.

Since I already had such a cushy job in London the expectation was that I would continue on that pathway. That was not to be as circumstances would have it. It is not easy to move on despite the odds. Once your mind set is in a certain direction it is difficult to stop and go back to the drawing board. There are so many things to think about. Mostly though I must admit that the main focus has been on what others would think. That held me in a position of hesitancy for a long time. Not making any direct decision, not following through and basically procrastinating about things. Procrastination does no tbring positive results. One must be proactive.

One day it suddenly dawned on me that I was making excuses. I needed to take action. Then a further thought came to me. The book is actually my action plan for moving forward. As I write the book everything will be made clearer and by the time it is finished my plan should be partway to being completed.

Mapping the success route is an essential tool for development. It should help us to reflect on what we deem success to be. What success looks like will also be at the forefront of our strategy. We will then review our pathway to success using a simple functional framework. For a number of us it is our spirituality that has kept us going through thick and thin in this ever-changing culture. When life gets difficult it is that faith by the grace of God that brings us back from the edge giving us the strength to persevere. Most have had their fair share of successes and failure some more than others. It is very difficult to think of anyone who's never experienced a success or failure.

Whether minor or major it all counts towards our experiences and character building. Often plans are made with no thought that the outcome might not necessarily be what was anticipated. Success is usually met with applauds and encouragement. On the other hand when plans do not reach the anticipated outcome some give thought to blame others. Others make an effort to find why they fell short, while a number of individuals consider giving up. Whatever the associated thought processes are there is a clear need of each individual to be re-motivated in order to find will to move on.

1. Write down what 3 ideas of success looks like to you, e.g., becoming, an author, doctor and business owner.
    A.
    B.
    C.

2. What are the barriers to doing this, e.g., time, finance etc.?
    A.
    B.
    C.

    What are the benefits of doing this?
    A.
    B.
    C.

Before doing the next session give yourself a pep talk. No one is to blame for where I am right now. I will not blame myself. My focus is totally on my journey and me. Now remind yourself:

3. What is not going so well in your vision of success so far?
    A.
    B.
    C.

Finding the gap is not easy. Those of us who have gaps in our paths to success, we have a lot to learn from scriptural examples. Had it not been for the will of God and the partnership we have with Him our hope of stability and survival would have been very dim.

Growing in partnership with God is very simple if one chooses to communicate with Him and follow His guidance. In *Matthew 10:1-2* Jesus called his twelve chosen disciples to him and instructed them. He was sending them on a journey and gave them the authority to drive out evil spirits and to heal every disease and sickness they encountered. Jesus' plan for his disciples was very specific as we will see further on in the chapter. What does all this have to do with us? Despite the fact that He is no longer present in flesh we've been blessed with the power of prayer. Praying is considered direct communication with God the father and should be done through Jesus Christ the mediator. Therefore we can ask for Gods guidance in planning our progress.

It is important to find time during your day for prayer and communication to God. Find a private place with no interruptions. Prayer doesn't have to be long winded. Try not to repeat the same words all the time. Talk to God as if he is present. Be earnest, reverent and sincere and don't forget to give thanks. Jot down your key prayer words for prayer below.

A.

Praying the right words can be difficult for some. A good place to start would be to jot down words that reflect your needs. Your needs can include blessings, thankfulness, gratitude, forgiveness, repentance and whatever it is you are asking for. There are many examples of praying both in the Bible and in many books. Prayer is a personal thing and as such each individual might choose a different approach. Just as it is important to pray to God for His guidance it is equally essential to understand his instructions. The only way to gain clarity about what God wants from us is to take time to ask the Lord what direction we should take in our lives. Once we are satisfied in our hearts of what he wants from us; we can make our plans following his guidance and direction. By listening to the Lord in prayer we can further align ourselves with His specific purposes for our lives and therefore have greater success in reaching the goals He allows us. Goals should be realistic and reachable. Now set some goals:

1. Long Term or end result: e.g. where do you want to be in 5 years? Married with children? Own your home?
   A.
   B.

2. Short term goals/steps to getting there: e.g. If you want to be a Doctor, you must get through college, get a loan etc.

    A.

    B.

    C.

Our God give's clear instructions as outlined in *Matthew, 10: 5-14*. We should never doubt that God would give us clear instructions when we ask for it. He has demonstrated that he will in so many different ways. Jesus sent out his twelve disciples with the following set of instructions. Look how specific his instructions were. *'You must not go among the Gentiles or enter any town of the Samaritans. Instead go to the lost sheep of Israel and as you go, preach the following message: 'The kingdom of heaven is near.'* They were asked to heal the sick, raise the dead, cleanse those suffering from a disorder called leprosy, and drive out demons. He further instructed them, *'freely you have received, and freely* you should give'.

Additional instructions given include; *'do not take with you any gold, silver or copper in your belts; take no bag for the journey, and no extra items of clothing, or sandals or a staff. For, the worker is worth his keep'.* I must admit that some of these instructions would be hard to follow in this era. As humans today we would surely worry about what to wear, money to buy food etc., cell phones and iPods.

He continues, *'whatever town or village you enter, search for some worthy person there and stay at his house until you leave. On entering the home, give it your greeting. And if the home deserves, let your peace rest on it. If it does not deserve, let your peace return to you. If anyone will not welcome you or listen to your words, shake the dust off your feet when you leave the home or town.* Can you see how clear this instruction is? This reminds me of the situation Montserrat in England found themselves in 1997 and 1998. Half of us had no clue what we were coming to, where we would live, eat or sleep. In spite of this we put our trust somewhere, hopefully it was in God, and we came through faith. In the same way we must continue trusting in God to help us along the way as we try to reach our goals. We are surely going to face different challenges. It cannot be over emphasized how important it is for our goals, plans and instructions to come directly out of our time in prayer with God. We must never forget that we can go to Him in prayer with confidence asking for his strength and grace to achieve our goals. Most of all we need to be sure that our plans are also a part of God's will, hence the importance of prayer and communication with Him. *Rejoice always, pray without ceasing, giving thanks in all circumstances; for that is the will of God in Christ Jesus for you. 1Thessalonians 5: 16-18.* If God does not agree with our plans we will find it difficult to progress. We may not be able to recognize the pitfalls ahead of us. However, God can help us avoid things that can be detrimental. He will not allow our plans to continue unless it is to His glory.

God has promised to empower us to achieve those goals that are aligned with His will. *Isaiah 40:31* reminds us that *they who wait upon the Lord shall renew their strength; they shall mount up with wings like eagles; they shall run and not be weary; they shall walk and not faint.* Can you doubt that this is the greatest assurance and confidence we have in approaching God? *If we ask for his support regarding anything that is in accord with his will, he hears us. And if we know that He hears, whatever we ask, we know that we will have the petitions that we have asked of Him. 1 John 5:14-15.*

Life is never as straightforward as we would like it to be. By this time I am sure we are all aware of this. This knowledge sometimes leaves us feeling frustrated. We feel the need to be re-motivated and to be, energized.

While some people are very good at dealing with this frustration others may give up or give in and become depressed and even consider isolating themselves from others. Additionally we may blame others for our setbacks in life with no regard or thought for the simple fact that it could be God's will that our plans do not reach fruition at this particular time or never does for that matter.

Whatever the reason for plans not being realized, not being successful or not as we anticipated they would be; it is important to communicate with God. Give him the opportunity to direct or redirect our paths as He purpose. Look at the reminder in *Romans 8:28. And we know that all things work together for good to them that love God, to them who are called according to His purpose.* As humans we often require an explanation for things that don't go to plan but God does not work this way simply because he knows what is best for us. It often helps to delve into the scriptures to see how setbacks and challenges were dealt with.

In *Romans 1:9-10*, Paul made a plan to visit some churches but had a number of setbacks and challenges on the way. Paul's setbacks came not only from people around him but he was also restricted by God's sovereign plans. *1Thessalonians 2:18* further shows that after being kept by the Holy Spirit from preaching in the province of Asia, Paul and his companions travelled throughout the region of Phrygia and Galatia instead. Basically he engaged himself in other useful projects. Paul could have sat back and give up because his original plans was foiled. Imagine yourself in Paul's position. Have you ever had a set back? How did it make you feel? How did you address it?

What are the barriers to achieving your goals?

A.

B.

C.

But Paul still had work to do of course, for he had a plan didn't he? He didn't stop his work completely, sit back and do nothing or feel sorry for himself and blame others. This would have been counterproductive. Instead we are shown how through persistent prayer Paul remained responsive to the Holy Spirit's promptings. He was therefore able to redirect his goals in order to align his plans with God's greater purposes. *Acts 16:6.*

Further Resources

A. S. Cookson. The Man who came to London

Entrepreneur Business Academy.
www.the -eba.com

National Domestic Violence Hotline (USA)
available at www.the hotline.org (1-800 799 7233

Report Domestic Abuse –GOV.UK
Available at, www.gov.uk

Stephen R. Covey. Seven Habits of Highly effective People.

References

Bray, I. (2019). When Can I Apply for U.S. Citizenship? Retrieved from https://www.nolo.com/legal-encyclopedia/when-apply-us-citizenship-46704.html

Caribbean Families - Family Structure. (2019). Retrieved from https://family.jrank.org/pages/203/Caribbean-Families-Family-Structure.html

Caribbean Life in New York City: Sociocultural Dimensions - The Center for Migration Studies of New York (CMS). (2019). Retrieved from https://cmsny.org/publications/book-caribbean-life-in-new-york-city/

Culture of Montserrat - history, people, clothing, beliefs, food, customs, family, social, marriage. (2019).
Retrieved from https://www.everyculture.com/Ma-Ni/Montserrat.html

Culture of the Caribbean. (2019). Retrieved from https://en.m.wikipedia.org/wiki/Caribbean_culture

Facts About Montserrat. (2019). Retrieved from http://worldfacts.us/Montserrat.htm

Greenaway. S. (2019). A Travellers Guide to Montserrat Dialect. Montserrat English.

Greenaway. S. (2011) Montserrat in England: Dynamics of Culture. iUniverse.

Immigrant and Non-Immigrant Visa Types - Find Law. (2019). Retrieved from https://immigration.findlaw.com/visas/immigrant-and-non-immigrant-visa-types.html

Indigenous peoples of the Americas. (2019). Retrieved from https://en.m.wikipedia.org/wiki/Indigenous_peoples_of_the_Americas

List of Caribbean countries by population. (2019). Retrieved from https://en.m.wikipedia.org/wiki/List_of_Caribbean_countries_by_population

Montserrat. (2019). Retrieved from https://en.m.wikipedia.org/wiki/Montserrat

New York's People & Cultures | Museums, Historic Sites. (2019). Retrieved from https://www.iloveny.com/things-to-do/culture/people-cultures/

The Immigrant Visa Process. (2019). Retrieved from https://travel.state.gov/content/travel/en/us-visas/immigrate/the-immigrant-visa-process.html

U.S. Department of Homeland Security (DHS), Office of Immigration Statistics. 2018. 2017 Yearbook of Immigration Statistics. Washington, DC: DHS Office of Immigration Statistics. **Available online**.

Williams et al. (2018). Next Level LIFT: Encouraging the Emerging Faith-Based Entrepreneur. Available on amazon.com

Printed in the United States
By Bookmasters